World of Whales

Humpback Whales

by Jenna Lee Gleisner

Bullfrog Books

Ideas for Parents and Teachers

Bullfrog Books let children practice reading informational text at the earliest reading levels. Repetition, familiar words, and photo labels support early readers.

Before Reading
- Discuss the cover photo. What does it tell them?
- Look at the picture glossary together. Read and discuss the words.

Read the Book
- "Walk" through the book and look at the photos. Let the child ask questions. Point out the photo labels.
- Read the book to the child, or have him or her read independently.

After Reading
- Prompt the child to think more. Ask: Humpback whales live in groups called pods. Can you name other animals that live in groups?

Bullfrog Books are published by Jump!
5357 Penn Avenue South
Minneapolis, MN 55419
www.jumplibrary.com

Copyright © 2024 Jump! International copyright reserved in all countries. No part of this book may be reproduced in any form without written permission from the publisher.

Library of Congress Cataloging-in-Publication Data

Names: Gleisner, Jenna Lee, author.
Title: Humpback whales / by Jenna Lee Gleisner.
Description: Minneapolis, MN: Jump!, Inc., [2024]
Series: World of whales | Includes index.
Audience: Ages 5–8
Identifiers: LCCN 2022051272 (print)
LCCN 2022051273 (ebook)
ISBN 9798885245951 (hardcover)
ISBN 9798885245968 (paperback)
ISBN 9798885245975 (ebook)
Subjects: LCSH: Humpback whale—Juvenile literature.
Classification: LCC QL737.C424 G59 2024 (print)
LCC QL737.C424 (ebook)
DDC 599.5/25—dc23/eng/20221026
LC record available at https://lccn.loc.gov/2022051272
LC ebook record available at https://lccn.loc.gov/2022051273

Editor: Katie Chanez
Designer: Emma Almgren-Bersie

Photo Credits: Maria T Hoffman/Shutterstock, cover; Philip Thurston/iStock, 1; Hello Adobe/Shutterstock, 3; KenCanning/iStock, 4, 11; miblue5/iStock, 5; Imagine Earth Photography/Shutterstock, 6–7; jeremyborkat/iStock, 8–9, 23m; Claude Huot/Shutterstock, 10; Kevin Schafer/Alamy, 12–13, 23br; John Tunney/Shutterstock, 14–15, 23tl; Tomas Kotouc/Shutterstock, 16–17, 23bm; Arterra Picture Library/Alamy, 18, 23tr; Chase Dekker/Shutterstock, 19; Kara Capaldo/iStock, 20–21, 23bl; Marti Bug Catcher/Shutterstock, 24.

Printed in the United States of America at Corporate Graphics in North Mankato, Minnesota.

Table of Contents

Spray and Splash 4
Parts of a Humpback Whale 22
Picture Glossary 23
Index 24
To Learn More 24

Spray and Splash

Water sprays into the air.

It came from a humpback whale!

The whale swims in the ocean.

Its fins are long.

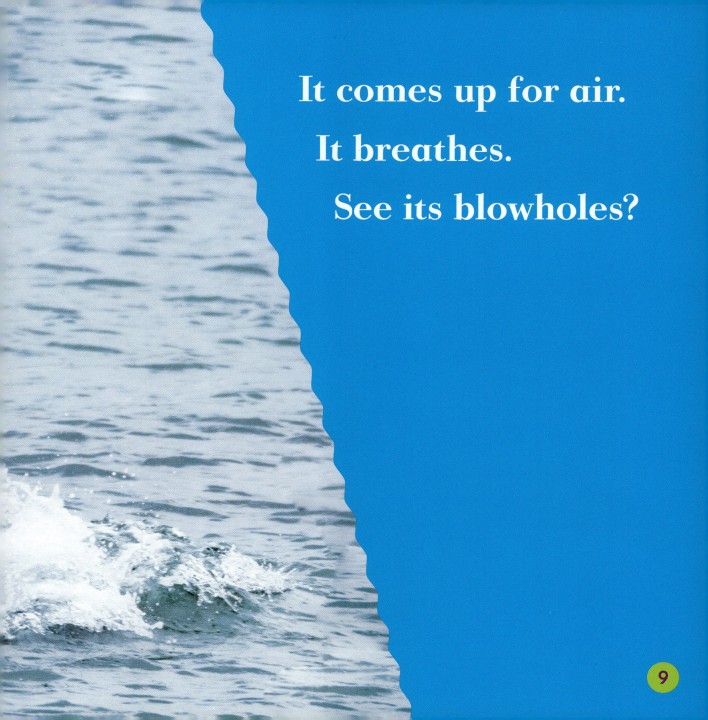

It comes up for air.
It breathes.
See its blowholes?

The whale jumps.
We see its grooves.

groove

Splash!

It eats a lot.

How?

It gulps water.

Baleen strain water out.
Fish stay in.
Yum!

A pod swims. They talk to each other. How? They make many sounds.

The pod hunts.
They make a bubble net.
Fish get stuck in it.

bubble net

The whales swim up.
They get the fish!

They swim to warm water.

Why?

Moms have calves.

They grow up in the pod.

Parts of a Humpback Whale

Humpback whales can be up to 60 feet (18 meters) long. That is almost as long as two school buses! Take a look at the parts of a humpback whale.

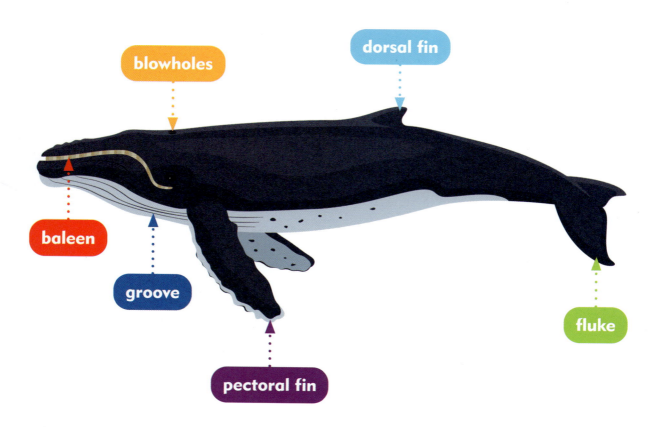

Picture Glossary

baleen
Plates in a whale's mouth that filter water and food.

blowholes
Nostrils on top of whale and dolphin heads used for breathing.

bubble net
A curtain of air bubbles humpback whales make to trap fish.

calves
Young whales.

pod
A group of whales.

strain
To separate solids out of liquids.

Index

baleen 14
blowholes 9
bubble net 18
calves 20
eats 13
fins 6
fish 14, 18, 19
grooves 10
hunts 18
ocean 6
pod 17, 18, 20
swims 6, 17, 19, 20

To Learn More

Finding more information is as easy as 1, 2, 3.

❶ Go to www.factsurfer.com
❷ Enter "humpbackwhales" into the search box.
❸ Choose your book to see a list of websites.